In addition to all the language forms which are used again at this level of the series, the main verb forms and tenses used at Level Four are:

- present perfect continuous verbs, past perfect verbs, *was/were going to,* passive verbs (simple aspects only and with available modal verbs), conditional clauses (using the 'second' or 'improbable' or 'hypothetical future' conditional) and further phrasal verbs

- modal verbs: *should* and *ought to* (to give advice or expressing desirability), *used to* (to describe past habits, states and routines), *must* and *can't* (to express (deduced) likelihood), and *may* and *might* (to express possibility or uncertainty), *could* (to express hypothetical ability), *would* (to express willingness) and *had better* (to give advice).

Specific attention is paid to vocabulary development in the Vocabulary Work exercises at the end of the book. These exercises are aimed at training students to enlarge their vocabulary systematically through intelligent reading and effective use of a dictionary.

To the student:

Dictionary Words:

- As you read this book, you will find that some words are in darker black ink than the others on the page. Look them up in your dictionary, if you do not already know them, or try to guess the meaning of the words first, and then look them up later, to check.

Saturday, 13 June 1942

On Friday, 12 June, I woke up early at six o'clock; it was my birthday. I'm not **allowed** to get up then, so I had to wait until quarter to seven. Then I went down to the dining-room, where Moortje, my cat, welcomed me. At seven I went in to Mummy and Daddy, and then to the sitting-room for my presents. The nicest present was *you* – my diary! There was a bunch of roses on the table, and lots more flowers and presents arrived for me during the day. Daddy and Mummy gave me a blue blouse, a game and a bottle of fruit juice which tastes quite like wine!

At school, I **shared** out some cakes with my friends, and I was allowed to choose the game that we played in the sports lesson. Afterwards, all my friends danced round me in a circle and sang 'Happy Birthday'.

Saturday, 20 June 1942

It's strange, writing a diary. Of course, I've written things before, but who will be interested in the thoughts of a thirteen-year-old schoolgirl? Well, does it matter? I want to write, and I want to bring out so many things that lie deep in my heart.

I need a diary because I haven't got a friend. You won't believe that I am completely alone in the world! And I'm not. I have loving parents and a sixteen-year-old sister, a good home and about thirty people that I can call friends. There are plenty of boys who are interested in me too! But I haven't got that one, true friend who understands me. So this diary can be my new friend. Let's start with the story of my life.

My father – the best father in the world – was thirty-six when mother, who was then twenty-five. My sister born in Frankfurt-am-Main in Germany in 1926. allowed on 12 June, 1929. Because we are Jewish, we to Holland in 1933. My father is the manager of a company called Opteka, which makes things for the jam-making business.

After 1940 things were not so good any more. First the war started, and then the Germans arrived in Holland. Our freedom disappeared. Under the new German laws, Jews must wear a yellow star. Jews must walk everywhere. They can only do their shopping in 'Jewish Shops', and they must be indoors by eight o'clock at night. They must not even sit in their own gardens after that time. Jews cannot visit the theatre or the cinema. Jews cannot visit Christians, and their children must go to Jewish schools.

Sunday, 21 June 1942

Everyone at school is waiting to hear what happens next. Who will move up a class, and who will stay down? We're all trying to guess! I think my girlfriends and I will be OK, though we'll have to wait patiently to find out.

Most of my teachers like me, but old Mr Keesing gets angry with me because I often talk too much! He made me do some extra homework and write about 'Someone Who Talks Too Much'.

Wednesday, 24 June 1942

It is so hot! Yesterday I had to walk to the dentist's from school in our lunch hour. I wish that we could go on a bus or a train, but of course us Jews are not allowed to do that. It was so far that I nearly

Margot and Anne with their father. Frankfurt, Germany, 1930.

fell asleep afterwards in the afternoon. They were kind at the dentist's, though, and gave me something to drink.

I wish I didn't have to go to school. I'm glad it's nearly the summer holidays; one more week and our **suffering** will be over!

But something amusing happened too yesterday. A boy called Hello Silberberg asked me to walk to school with him. Hello is sixteen, and tells lots of funny stories. He was waiting for me again this morning.

Wednesday, 1 July 1942

I haven't had time to write until today. Hello and I know each other quite well now. His parents are in Belgium. He came to Holland alone, and is living with his grandmother. He had a girlfriend called Ursula, but now that he's met me, he's not interested in her any more. I know her too – she's very sweet and very boring!

Hello came over on Sunday evening. He told me that his grandmother doesn't like our meetings. But on Wednesday nights, his grandmother thinks that he goes to woodwork lessons – he doesn't, so he'll be free to meet me! And he said that he wants to see me on Saturdays and Sundays too!

'But if your grandmother doesn't want you to meet me, you shouldn't do it behind her back!'

'Everything's allowed in love and war!'

Hello visited us yesterday to meet my Father and Mother. We had a big tea, and went out for a walk together later. It was ten past eight when he brought me home. Father was very angry because it is so dangerous to be out after eight o'clock. I promised to come home by ten to eight in future.

Sunday, 5 July 1942

My exam results were good! My parents are pleased, of course. And Margot had a brilliant report, as usual.

Father has been at home a lot lately, because he can't work at the business any more. It must be awful for him to feel that he's not needed there. Mr Kleiman and Mr Kugler are now the managers in the offices.

When we went out for a walk together a few days ago, Father said, 'We may have to go into hiding soon.'

'Why?' I asked him. 'Why are you talking about it already?'

'Well, Anne,' he said, 'you know that we've been making **stores** of food, clothes and furniture for more than a year now. The Germans could take everything away, and us too.' He was very serious.

'But when will we go?'

'Don't worry – we'll arrange everything. Just enjoy yourself while you can!'

Wednesday, 8 July 1942

It seems like years since Sunday morning. So much has happened – the whole world has turned upside down. But I'm alive, and that's the most important thing.

On Sunday afternoon we heard that the Germans were going to take Father away. We know what that means – to a **concentration camp**.

'Mother's gone to ask Mr van Daan about our hiding-place,' said Margot. Mr van Daan worked in the business with Daddy and is a good friend of his.

Then Margot told me later that there was a mistake – the

Johannes Kleiman and Victor Kugler. Amsterdam, 1945.

Germans had called her up, not Father. How can they take a girl of sixteen away from her family like that? But she's not going!

A hiding-place – where shall we hide? In the city? In the country? When, where, how ...? These questions were in my mind, though I couldn't ask them.

Margot and I started to pack. I packed the craziest things! This diary first, then handkerchiefs, schoolbooks, a comb and some old letters. Memories are more important to me than dresses.

Miep and her husband Jan came to help and share the work. They carried some bags of clothes away for us. Miep and Jan work for Father's company and they are our close friends. I slept for the last night in my own bed, and Mummy woke me up at five-thirty. We dressed in lots of clothes. No Jew would dare to leave the house with a suitcase!

At seven-thirty we left the house. I said goodbye to Moortje, my cat. The neighbours were going to look after her. We hurried to leave the house – we wanted to reach our hiding-place safely. It was the only thing that mattered.

More tomorrow.

Thursday, 9 July 1942

The hiding-place is in Father's office building. On the bottom floor is the **warehouse**, and next to it an entrance to the office, which is upstairs. There are two offices – a front one which is big and light, and a small dark one at the back. Not many people work in Father's offices, just Mr Kugler, Mr Kleiman, Miep and a twenty-three-year-old typist called Bep Voskuijl. Mr Voskuijl, Bep's father, works in the warehouse with two helpers, who don't know anything about us. From Mr Kugler's office at the back, you go up another four stairs and you come to the private office, which is very fine and has good furniture.

Up on the third floor is our 'Secret **Annexe**'. There are some **attics** for storage on the left, and on the right is the door to our hiding-place. It's surprising that there are so many rooms behind that small grey door. Margot and I share a small room, and Mother and Father's bedroom is also our sitting-room. Up the stairs again is a big light room which will be the kitchen and Mr and Mrs van Daan's bedroom. There is a very small room for Peter, their son, and another attic. So that's our lovely Annexe!

Friday, 10 July 1942

Let me continue the story. When we arrived at the warehouse, the Annexe was full of all the boxes that we had stored at the office for the last few months. No one could possibly sleep there unless we cleared it up. But Mother and Margot were really suffering, and they were too tired and unhappy to help. They just lay down on their beds, so Father and I did it all. We worked all day, until we were so tired that we fell into bed too. There was no hot meal, but we didn't care. We worked all the next day, too, which was Tuesday. Bep and Miep took our **ration** books to buy food.

It was only on Wednesday that I had time to think about the enormous change in my life. Now I've got a moment to tell you all about it, to realize what has happened, and what is still to happen.

Saturday, 11 July 1942

The others can't get used to the big clock outside which tells the time every quarter of an hour. But I like it, specially at night. I don't feel at home here yet. I don't hate it though. It is like a holiday in a strange little hotel. My bedroom was very empty

Plan of the Secret Annexe.

when I arrived, but I've stuck up pictures of my favourite film actors and actresses. It's a lot better now.

Margot and Mother are a bit better now too. Yesterday Mother cooked some soup for the first time, but she went downstairs to talk and forgot all about it! The beans were burnt black, and we couldn't get them out of the pot!

Last night, the four of us went down to the private office to listen to the news from the BBC in England on the radio. I was so frightened that I asked Father to take me back upstairs! I thought someone might hear it. We have to be very quiet at night.

Friday, 14 August 1942

I haven't written for a month now, but not much has happened. The van Daans arrived a day early, on July the 13th. The Germans were calling up a lot of people, and they thought it was safer to come early. Peter, their son, is a shy boy of almost sixteen. I don't think he will be a very interesting friend.

We all share our meals now, and after three days we began to feel like one big family! The van Daans told us a lot of news. People think we are escaping to Switzerland! Although one woman says that an army lorry took us away in the middle of the night! And another family say that they saw all four of us riding on our bikes early one morning!

Friday, 21 August 1942

Now our Secret Annexe is really secret! Mr Kugler has built a **bookcase** over our little entrance. It opens like a door.

It's a beautiful day outside, nice and hot. We can still enjoy it, lying on a bed in the attic.

Monday, 21 September 1942

Mrs van Daan is awful. She says that I talk too much. She won't save food in a dish – she leaves it in the cooking pot so that it gets spoiled. And she doesn't do any washing up.

Mr Kleiman brings me books to read, and I've begun my schoolwork. I'm working hard at French, and Peter is learning English. Pim – our name for father – wants me to help him with his Dutch lessons. He makes terrible mistakes! He and I are also working on our family **history**, and drawing our family tree, so I am learning about all my relations.

Mrs van Daan walked into the room just now. I shut the diary quickly.

'Anne, can't I just look at it?'

'No, Mrs van Daan.'

'Just the last page?'

'No, not even the last page, Mrs van Daan.'

I nearly died – that page was full of rude things about her!

Sunday, 27 September 1942

Mother and I had a 'discussion' today, but I burst into tears. I can't help it. Daddy is *always* nice to me, and he understands me much better. I feel that Mother and I are like strangers to each other.

Mrs van Daan is in a bad mood, and is locking all her things up. She thinks that I am spoilt, and always says, 'If Anne was my daughter . . .' I'm glad that I'm not!

Tuesday, 29 September 1942

Try to imagine this. We haven't got a bathroom, so we all take our water away to wash in different places! Peter goes in the office kitchen, which has a glass door. Mr van Daan carries his hot water upstairs so that he can be private. Mrs van Daan hasn't had a bath yet – she can't decide which is the best place for it! Father goes into the private office and Mother into the kitchen. Margot and I share the front office. We close the curtains and wash ourselves there in the dark!

On Wednesday someone was doing repairs in the office downstairs. We couldn't use the toilet or use water all day. Father and I found a suitable pot which we could all use as a toilet! We had to sit still all day and not say a word! That was the most difficult thing for me.

Thursday, 1 October 1942

Yesterday I was very frightened. At eight o'clock the doorbell suddenly rang. I thought that the Germans were coming to get us. But everybody said that someone only rang for a joke, or that maybe it was the postman, and I felt calm again.

Peter can be very funny sometimes. We both like to dress up in silly clothes. One evening, he put on one of his mother's tight dresses, and I wore his suit! Everyone laughed so much!

Miep bought new skirts for Margot and me at The Bijenkorf.★ They look like potato bags!

★ A large shop in the centre of Amsterdam.

Friday, 9 October 1942

The news is very bad today. The Germans are taking away many of our Jewish friends. They are sent to concentration camps at Westerbork, or even further away. We think many of them are murdered there. I feel terrible. The English radio says that the Germans are killing them with gas. Perhaps that's the quickest way to die. Perhaps you don't suffer so much that way.

Tuesday, 20 October 1942

My hand is still shaking as I write this. Two hours ago we heard an awful noise at our bookcase door. The knocking didn't stop, and someone was pushing and pulling at the door. Perhaps they had come to **arrest** us! We were white with fear! But at last we heard Mr Kleiman's voice. 'Open up, it's me!' The door was stuck, and he couldn't open it.

We had a good time on Monday. Miep and Jan spent the night with us. We cooked specially for them, and the meal tasted wonderful.

Monday, 9 November 1942

Yesterday was Peter's sixteenth birthday. He had a game and a cigarette lighter – he doesn't smoke much, but the lighter looks good!

There was a big surprise too. Mr van Daan heard that the English have reached Tunis, Algiers, Casablanca and Oran. It is not the end of the war yet, but perhaps we can hope for the end now. Perhaps it will soon be history.

Well, what about food in the Annexe? A man brings bread

Johannes Kleiman next to the bookcase.

every day, a very nice friend of Mr Kleiman's. And we've stored a hundred tins of food here. We can buy ration books on the black market*, and we've also bought three hundred pounds of beans. We decided to move them to the attic, and Peter was given the job. He succeeded in getting five sacks upstairs, but the sixth sack burst, and a river of beans poured downstairs! I was standing at the bottom of the stairs. Peter couldn't stop laughing when he saw me

* When people buy and sell things unofficially, this is called the 'black market'. The black market usually works when food, clothes or other things are hard to find and very expensive.

in a sea of brown beans. Unfortunately though, the beans are very small and have disappeared into all the holes. Whenever we go upstairs now, we look for a few more beans!

Tuesday, 10 November 1942

Great news! Another person is coming to live here. Eight is no more difficult than seven, and it is so dangerous for Jews now. We have chosen a dentist called Alfred Dussel. He seems to be nice. Miep knows him, and she will help him to get here. He will have to sleep in my room though, and Margot will have to move in with our parents. We'll ask him to fill the holes in our teeth!

Tuesday, 17 November 1942

Mr Dussel has arrived. Everything went smoothly. He came to the warehouse, and Miep asked him to take off his coat, so that no one could see the yellow star. Then she brought him to the private office. He still had no idea where he was going, or what was going to happen! When she opened our bookcase door, he was so surprised! He thought we had left the country. We were waiting around the table, ready to welcome him with a drink.

After lunch he slept for a short time, put away his things, and joined us for tea. We gave him the list of rules for the Secret Annexe that the van Daans had written.

GUIDE TO THE SECRET ANNEXE
For Jews and other people without homes

Open all year round: Near to the centre of Amsterdam, but in a quiet street with trees.

Price: Free.

Food: Low fat.

Water: In the bathroom (sorry, no fixed bath) and also on some of the walls.

Space for storing things: Plenty.

Private radio: For all guests after 6 p.m. But you must never listen to the news on German radio stations, only music.

Rest hours: From 10 p.m. to 7.30 a.m.; 10.15 a.m. on Sundays. This is for your safety. The Management may also ask you to rest at other times too.

Use of language: Speak softly at all times, and not in German.

Exercise: Every day.

Lessons: Offered in English, French, and other subjects.

Singing: Only softly, and after 6 p.m.

Mealtimes: Breakfast 9 a.m. (11.30 a.m. on Sundays and holidays).

               Lunch: A light meal from 1.15 p.m. to 1.45 p.m.

               Dinner: Sometimes a hot meal, sometimes not. The time of dinner changes because of radio news broadcasts.

Bath: The moveable bath can be used by all guests after 9 a.m. on Sundays. You may take your bath in the bathroom, kitchen, private office or front office.

The end

Thursday, 19 November 1942

It's true, Mr Dussel is a very nice man. He's willing to share a room with me, although I don't really like sharing my things with a stranger. But we all have to give up something here. 'If we can save just one of our friends, we will be doing something to help,' says Father. He's right.

Mr Dussel has told us a lot about the outside world. The news is terrible. The **authorities** have taken away so many friends and people we know to concentration camps. Army cars go round the streets day and night to arrest people. They're looking for Jews; they knock on every door, and ask whether any Jews live there. When they find a Jewish family, they take everybody away. They even pay money for information. In the evenings, when it's dark, I often see long lines of innocent people walking on and on. Sick people, old people, children, babies – all walking to their deaths.

We are very lucky here. I feel bad, sleeping in a warm bed when our dearest friends are suffering so badly. And only because they are Jews.

Saturday, 28 November 1942

Mr Dussel complains about me all the time. And they said that he liked children! He complains to Mother, and then she is angry with me too. I think about it all in bed at night. Am I so bad? I either laugh or cry, then I fall asleep, wanting to be different. It's very confusing.

Tuesday, 22 December 1942

The Annexe was delighted to hear that we are all getting an extra quarter pound of butter for Christmas. We are each going to cook something with butter.

Mr Dussel says 'Quiet, quiet!' to me all night, even if I just turn over in bed. But *he* gets up early on Sundays and puts on the light to do his exercises.

Yes, we all have to be very sensible here and not get angry! But I would love to lock the door, or hide his clothes, or do something not at all sensible!

Wednesday, 13 January 1943

Terrible things are happening outside. People are being pulled out of their homes and arrested. They have to leave with only a small bag and a little money, but even that is stolen from them. Families are separated. When children come home from school, their parents have disappeared. The sons of Christian families in Holland are also sent to Germany. Everyone is frightened. Every night, there are air **raids**. Hundreds of aeroplanes fly over Holland to drop bombs on German cities. Every hour, hundreds or maybe thousands of people are killed in Russia and Africa. The whole world is at war. Although the **Allies** are doing better now, the end of the war is nowhere in sight.

We are luckier than millions of people. It is quiet and safe here. We have money to buy food. We're selfish – we talk about 'after the war', and we look forward to new clothes and shoes. But we should save our money to share with others later.

The children round here only have thin shirts and wooden shoes – no coats or socks. There is no one to help them. They are always hungry, and ask people on the streets for bread. I could tell you more about the suffering that the war has brought, but it would make me too sad. All we can do is to wait patiently until it is over.

Saturday, 27 February 1943

Pim thinks there will be an **invasion** by the Allies at any time now. Churchill★ was seriously ill, but now he's getting better.

★ Winston Churchill, who led the British Government during World War II.

We are sharing our butter a different way now. Everyone gets their own piece on their own plate. But it's not done right – the van Daans make breakfast for everyone, and give themselves the biggest share of the butter. My parents are too frightened to argue, unfortunately.

Wednesday, 10 March 1943

I could hear the guns all last night. I am always frightened of shooting, and I usually climb into Father's bed to feel safe. The guns are really loud, and you can't hear your own voice.

One night, there were strange noises inside the Annexe. Peter went up to the attic and found – guess what? An army of enormous rats!

Friday, 2 April 1943

I'm in trouble again! Last night, I was lying in bed and waiting for Father to come and say my **prayers** with me. Mother came into the room, and asked gently, 'Anne, Daddy isn't ready? Shall I listen to your prayers tonight?'

'No, Mummy,' I said.

Mother got up, stood by my bed for a moment, then slowly walked to the door. Suddenly she turned round, and her face was full of pain. She said, 'I don't want to be angry with you. I can't make you love me!' A few tears fell down her cheeks as she went out of the door.

I lay still. I knew that it was cruel to say that, but I couldn't give her any other answer. I feel very sorry for her. She's pushed me away from her with her unkind jokes.

She cried for half the night, and didn't sleep. Father doesn't look at me, but I know what he is thinking: 'How can you be so unkind? How dare you make your mother so sad?'

But I can't apologise.

Tuesday, 27 April 1943

Everyone in the Annexe is still **quarrelling**. There are air raids and bombs every night, and nobody can sleep well.

Our food is terrible. We have plain bread and coffee – not real coffee – for breakfast. We have lettuce or green vegetables, and bad potatoes. That's all.

Saturday, 1 May 1943

Yesterday was Dussel's birthday. He pretended that he wasn't interested, but when Miep arrived with a large bag of presents from his friends, he was as excited as a child! He had chocolate, eggs, butter, oranges and books. He arranged them on the table and left them there for three days, the silly old fool!

He already has plenty of food. We found bread, cheese, jam and eggs in his cupboard. He hasn't given us anything, but we've shared everything with him.

Sunday, 13 June 1943

Father wrote something for my birthday – it's very funny! It's about me, and my hard life in the Annexe, under the authority of parents who are always telling me what to do! I had some lovely presents too, specially a big book of Greek and Roman stories, and sweets from everyone – people gave me some from the last of their stores.

Tuesday, 15 June 1943

Next month we have to give back our radio to the authorities. It's an official rule, and all over the country people are trying to find an old radio to give in so that they can keep their real radios in secret. It's a shame that we have to give in our beautiful big radio, but Mr Kleiman will give us a 'baby' radio which he has hidden at home. We'll put it upstairs. It's not allowed, of course, but we're not allowed to be here either! Our radio with its wonderful voice really helps us. We tell ourselves, 'Let's try to be brave and **cheerful**. Things must get better!'

Friday, 16 July 1943

There was a break-in last night, a real one! This morning, Peter went down to the warehouse and saw that the doors were open on to the street. We stayed quiet, and didn't use any water or do anything to make a noise. We waited until eleven-thirty, when Mr Kleiman came upstairs. He told us that burglars had broken in and stolen some money. Luckily, they didn't find much so they soon went next door to look there.

The Allies are arriving in Sicily!

Monday, 19 July 1943

A lot of bombs fell on North Amsterdam on Sunday. Whole streets went in the raid, and they can't even dig out all the bodies yet. They've already counted two hundred people dead, and many more are hurt. The hospitals are full.

Monday, 26 July 1943

There was a terrible bombing raid yesterday. It started at about two-thirty in the afternoon. Margot and I were upstairs, but the guns were so loud that we went down again. The house shook, and the bombs kept on falling. I was holding my 'escape bag'. But walking on the streets is as dangerous as an air raid on the Annexe. I know that I can't really leave. After half an hour the planes flew away, and the smell of fire was everywhere. There was thick smoke over the city, like fog.

Later, after dinner, there was another raid. The bombs came down again like rain, and we heard from British reports that Schiphol Airport was bombed. We could hear the noise of the planes all the time, and we were very frightened. My legs were still shaking when I lay in bed that night.

At midnight, more planes! I ran to father's bed and did not fall asleep in my own bed until half-past two.

But at seven o'clock in the morning we heard some wonderful news about Italy! Mussolini has gone, and the King of Italy is leading the government there now.

Tuesday, 3 August 1943

We just had a third air raid. I am trying to be brave. Mrs van Daan used to say, 'Let them fall!' Now she is the most cowardly of us all. She was shaking like a leaf this morning, and even burst into tears.

Our bodies are very stiff now. We stopped our exercise programme a long time ago.

Friday, 10 September 1943

Every time I write to you, something special has happened. Usually, it's unpleasant. But this time, it's wonderful! The news was broadcast that Italy is out of the war! The British are now in Naples. The Germans are in North Italy.

But there is some very bad news too. Mr Kleiman is going to have a very difficult operation on his stomach, and he'll have to stay in hospital for at least four weeks. He's so brave! He's always cheerful and smiling, although he's usually in pain.

Friday, 29 October 1943

Mr Kleiman is out of hospital now, but his stomach is still bad. He had to go home again today because he wasn't well.

Mr van Daan has sold his wife's best winter coat. She wanted to keep the money to buy new clothes after the war. Mr van Daan could not make her understand that the money has to be used for the Annexe. They shouted and screamed at each other – it was terrible.

I'm OK, but I'm not hungry at the moment. People say, 'You look awful, Anne!' Sundays are specially bad. It is deathly quiet then. I feel as though I am being pulled down into hell. I am a bird without wings who can't escape. A voice inside me cries, 'Let me out! I want to go into the fresh air. I want to hear people laughing!' I don't answer the voice, but just lie down on the sofa. Sleep makes time go more quickly.

Wednesday, 3 November 1943

We've decided to start our fire at seven-thirty on Sunday mornings, instead of five-thirty. I think it's dangerous. The neighbours may see the smoke, and what will they think? The curtains are a problem too. They cover the windows completely, but sometimes someone here will decide to take a little look outside. Everyone complains, but the answer is, 'Oh, nobody will notice.' That's how things start to get dangerous.

We are not quarrelling so much. Only Dussel and the van Daans are enemies at the moment. Dussel talks about Mrs van Daan as 'that stupid cow', and she calls him 'an old woman'!

Monday evening, 8 November 1943

We all have different moods here, up and down. And my mood is sad now. Miep says that we are peaceful here. But it's like a small circle of blue sky. We eight people in the Annexe are in that circle, but all around us are dark clouds and danger. The circle is getting smaller, and the darkness closer. If we could fly up into that blue sky, into heaven . . . Oh circle, open wide and let us out!

Sunday, 2 January 1944

This morning I read through some of the old pages in my diary. I was very ashamed when I saw what I had written about Mother. Why did I feel so angry then? Why did I hate her so much? It was true that she didn't understand me. But I didn't understand her either. I'm older and wiser now, and Mother is not so nervous. We try not to quarrel with each other. But I can't love her like a child any more.

Thursday, 6 January 1944

I realized what's wrong with Mother. She says that she sees us more as her friends, not her daughters. That's nice, but a friend is not the same as a mother.

I think the changes in my body are wonderful. Whenever I have my **period** (three times now), it's like a sweet secret inside me. There is pain, and mess, but I look forward to it again.

I need a friend, and I'm going to try Peter. I want badly to talk to someone. I had a chance to talk to him yesterday; I looked into his dark blue eyes and it gave me a wonderful feeling.

That night in bed I cried and cried. Must I *ask* Peter to be my friend? I don't love him, but I do need him. If the van Daans had a daughter, it would be just the same with her. So I've decided to visit Peter more often, and to make him talk to me.

Wednesday, 12 January 1944

I'm crazy about dance at the moment! I practise my steps every evening, and I've made myself a modern dance dress from Mother's clothes. I tried to turn my tennis shoes into dance shoes, but it didn't work. All the exercise is helping – I'm not nearly so stiff now!

Saturday, 15 January 1944

I won't tell you all the details of our quarrels in the Annexe. But we are not sharing our food in the same way now – we've got our own stores of meat and oil, and we even cook our own potatoes. Mother made a wish, 'I don't want to see Mr van Daan's face for two whole weeks.' Unfortunately, her wish is not likely to come

Edith Frank, May 1935.

true. Does everyone who shares a house become like this? Or are we just unlucky?

Thursday, 3 February 1944

Everybody is thinking about the Allied invasion! What will happen to us if the British invade Holland. The Germans say that they will let the water from the sea into the country.*

Each person has his or her own idea.

'We'll have to walk through the water.'

'Don't be silly! We'll have to try and swim. We'll swim underwater, and then nobody will see that we are Jews!'

'Oh, rubbish! Can ladies swim when rats are biting their legs?'

Next question: when the invasion comes, will the authorities make everybody leave Amsterdam?

'We'll leave the city with all the other people.'

'No, we mustn't go outside! The Germans will send everyone to die in Germany.'

'All right, we'll stay here. Let's ask Miep for some extra blankets. And some more food. We've got about sixty-five pounds of beans at the moment, and fifty tins of vegetables.'

'What's in the stores, Mother? Tell us.'

'Ten tins of fish, forty tins of milk, three bottles of oil, four jars of butter, four jars of fruit, twenty jars of tomatoes and nine pounds of rice. That's it.'

Our stores are still quite good. But we do have to feed the people in the office too.

'Let's make little bags for our money that we can hide in our clothes if we have to leave here.'

---

* Holland is very flat, and the water is carefully controlled. Once, most of the land was naturally under water.

And so it goes on all day. That's all I hear – invasion, invasion, only invasion. I'm very calm about it. I don't care now whether I live or die. I'll just keep on with my work and hope that everything will be all right in the end.

Wednesday, 16 February 1944

I had to go up into the attic, through Peter's room, to get some potatoes today. When I was going up the stairs, he stood up and took my arm.

'I'll go,' he said. But I told him that it wasn't necessary.

On my way down, I asked him, 'What are you studying?'

'French,' he replied. I asked if I could look at his lessons. Then I sat down on the sofa, and began to explain some French to him. We went on talking pleasantly about other things too, and finally he spoke about the picture of film actors on his wall. It's the one that I gave him, and he likes it very much.

'Shall I give you a few more?' I asked him.

'No,' he replied. 'I prefer this one. I look at it every day, and all the people in it have become my friends.'

Peter needs love, too. That's why he holds Mouschi the cat so tightly.

Friday, 18 February 1944

Whenever I go upstairs, it's always so that I can see *him*. I have something to look forward to now, and life here is better.

Mother doesn't like me going up there. She says that I should leave Peter alone. She always looks at me oddly when I go to Peter's room. When I come down again, she asks me where I've been.

Peter van Daan.

Wednesday, 23 February 1944

The weather is wonderful, and I feel better. Almost every morning, I go up to the attic for some fresh air – we can open the window there and look out. This morning, Peter was up there too. He came over to where I was sitting on the floor. The two of us looked out at the blue sky, at the tree and at the birds flying through the air. It was so beautiful that we couldn't speak. We stayed like this for a long time.

'How can I be sad when there is the sun and the sky?' I asked myself. God wants us to be happy and to see the beauty of this world. It will help us in all our troubles.

Sunday, 27 February 1944

I think about Peter from morning to night. I dream about him, and see his face when I wake up.

I feel that Peter and I are not really very different, although we seem to be on the outside. We both have strong feelings inside, which are difficult to control. Neither of us feels that we have a mother. His mother isn't serious; mine is interested in my life but she doesn't understand me at all.

Saturday, 4 March 1944

This was the first Saturday for months that wasn't boring. It was because of Peter. I joined the French lesson that Father was giving him. I was in heaven, sitting on Father's chair, close to Peter.

Afterwards, we talked together until lunch-time. Whenever I

leave the room after a meal, Peter says – if no one else can hear him – 'Goodbye, Anne – I'll see you later.'

Oh, I'm so happy! Perhaps he does love me! And it's so good to talk to him.

Friday, 10 March 1944

We have more troubles now. Miep is ill, and Mr Kleiman is still away from work with his bad stomach. Bep is trying to do everything on her own.

Last night, somebody knocked on the wall next door while we were having dinner. We were very nervous all evening.

The police have taken Mr M. away. He's the man who sells us potatoes, butter and jam on the black market. It's terrible for him and also for us. He has five young children and another baby coming.

Tuesday, 14 March 1944

I'm sitting at the van Daan's table with a handkerchief over my mouth. Why? Let me start at the beginning. They've arrested the people who bring our ration tickets, so we don't have any fats or oils. Miep and Mr Kleiman are ill again, and Bep can't go shopping for us. The food is awful. Lunch today is potatoes and some very old vegetables out of bottles. They smell terrible, which is why I have the handkerchief! We've got to eat them too – I feel sick when I think about it! Half the potatoes have gone bad, and we have to throw them away.

If life here was pleasant, the food would not matter so much. But it's the fourth year of the war, and we are all in bad moods.

Saturday, 18 March 1944

I've written so much about myself and my feelings, so why shouldn't I write about sex, too? Parents are very strange about sex. They should tell their sons and daughters everything at the age of twelve. But instead of that, they send them out of the room when anyone talks about sex, and the children have to try and find out everything by themselves. Then, later, the parents think that the children already know it all, but usually they don't!

Soon after I was eleven, they told me about periods. But I didn't know where the blood came from, or what it was for. When I was twelve and a half, one of my friends told me some more. She told me what a man and a woman do together. Well, I had already guessed! I was quite proud of myself! She also told me that babies don't come out of their mothers' stomachs. Where everything goes in is where the baby comes out!

Children hear about sex in bits and pieces, and that isn't right.

Although it's Saturday, I'm not bored! I've been up in the attic with Peter. I sat there dreaming with my eyes closed, and it was wonderful.

Sunday, 19 March 1944

Yesterday was a very important day for me. At five o'clock I put on the potatoes to cook, and Mother gave me some sausage to give to Peter. But he wouldn't take the sausage, and I thought it was because of the awful quarrel that we had recently. Suddenly, my eyes filled with tears. I took the plate back to Mother and went into the toilet to cry.

I decided to talk to Peter. After the washing up, I went to his room. We stood by the open window as it grew dark – it's much

Miep Gies and Bep Voskuijl. Amsterdam, 1945.

easier to talk like that. He didn't refuse the sausage because of our argument, but because he didn't want to look too greedy! Then we talked about so much together. It felt good; it was the most wonderful evening I've ever had in the Annexe.

We talked about our parents, and our problems with them. I told him how I cry in bed. He said that he goes up to the attic when he is angry. We talked all about our feelings. And it was just as good as I imagined!

We talked about the year 1942, and how different we are now. He thought that I was a noisy, annoying girl at first! I thought that he was uninteresting! I told him that we are like two sides of the same coin. I am noisy and he is quiet. But also that I too like peace and quiet. I said that I understand why he goes away to be alone sometimes. And that I'd like to help him when he argues with his parents.

'But you always help me!' he said.

'How?' I asked, very surprised.

'Because you're always cheerful.'

That was the nicest thing he said all evening. He must love me now as a friend, and I'm so grateful and happy for that.

Wednesday, 22 March 1944

Things are getting more and more wonderful here. I think that true love may be happening in the Annexe! Everyone has made jokes about us, saying that we might get married if we are all in the Annexe long enough. Perhaps those jokes aren't so silly at all.

I'm sure now that Peter loves me too, but I don't know in what way. Does he just want a good friend, or a girlfriend, or a sister?

Oh, when I think about Saturday night – about our words, our voices – I feel very satisfied with myself. For the first time, I don't want to change anything that I said.

Thursday, 23 March 1944

Our black market ration book men are out of prison now, so things are better here.

Yesterday a plane crashed quite near us, on top of a school. Luckily, there were no children inside. There was a small fire, and two people were killed. The men inside the plane were able to get out in time, but the Germans shot them immediately. Local people were so angry – it was a cowardly, horrible thing to do! We – the ladies of the Annexe – were very frightened. I hate the sound of guns.

Tuesday, 28 March 1944

Mother is trying to stop me going up to Peter's room. She says that Mrs van Daan is jealous. Perhaps she's jealous too. Father is happy about it; he's glad that we're friends. Mother thinks that Peter has fallen in love with me. I wish that it was true.

I do want to stay friends with Peter. We have our difficulties, but we have to fight against them, and in the end they will make everything more beautiful. When he rests his head on his arms and closes his eyes, he's still a child. When he plays with Mouschi, his cat, he's loving. When he carries the heavy potatoes for us, he's strong. When he watches the air raids, or walks through the dark house to look for burglars, he's brave. And when he doesn't know quite how to behave, he's sweet!

Wednesday, 29 March 1944

Mr Bolkestein, from the Government, was speaking on the Dutch broadcast from London. He said that after the war they wanted everybody's diaries and letters about the war – they would be an interesting part of history. I might be able to write a book called *The Secret Annexe*. People would think that it was a detective story! But seriously, ten years after the war people would find it very amusing to read about us, the Jews who were hiding. How we lived, what we ate, what we talked about. But although I tell you a lot about our lives, you still know very little about us. For example, how frightened the women are during the air raids. Last Sunday, 350 British planes dropped their bombs on Ijmuiden, so that the houses shook like grass in the wind. Or about the awful illnesses that people are catching here.

You know nothing about all this, and it would take me all day to describe it. People have to wait in line for vegetables and all kinds of other things too. Doctors can't visit the sick, since their cars and bikes are stolen at once. There are so many thieves around that you ask what has happened to the Dutch – why are they stealing so much? Little children, eight- and eleven-year-olds, break the windows of people's homes and steal whatever they can. People don't dare to leave the house even for five minutes, because everything may be gone when they return. The public phones are stolen, and all the parts of the electric clocks on the street corners too.

Everyone's hungry. A week's food ration doesn't even last two days. We're waiting for the Allied invasion, but it's so long coming. The men are sent to Germany, the children are ill or hungry, and everyone wears old clothes and broken shoes. It's too expensive to repair shoes, and if you give your shoes to a shoemender, you may never see them again.

263 Prinsengracht, Amsterdam. Front view.

Friday, 31 March 1944

Just imagine, it's still cold, but most people have had nothing to put on their fires for a month now. It sounds awful, doesn't it? But we are hopeful about the Russians, who are doing well. They've reached Poland now, and the Prut River in Romania. They're close to Odessa too.

The German Army has invaded Hungary. A million Jews still live there; there is no hope for them now.

Nothing special is happening here. Today is Mr van Daan's birthday. He received several presents and a cake. The cake wasn't perfect, because we can't buy the right things to make it with, but it tasted wonderful anyway!

People are not saying so much about Peter and me now. We're very good friends. We spend a lot of time together, and we talk about anything and everything. I couldn't talk to other boys like this. We even talked about periods. He thinks that women are

Mrs van Daan, Mr van Daan and Victor Kugler, left. Amsterdam, 1941.

strong enough to lose the blood, and that I am too. I wonder why he thinks that?

My life here is better now, much better. God has not left me, and He never will.

Monday, 3 April 1944

I'm going to describe our food rations. Food is a difficult and important problem not only for us in the Annexe, but for everyone in Holland, all of Europe and even further away.

We've lived here for twenty-one months, and often at any one time there was only one kind of food to eat. For example, one kind of vegetable or salad. We would eat it with potatoes, in every possible way that we could think of.

But now there are no vegetables at all. We have potatoes, and brown beans. We make soup – we still have some packets and stores to make dishes which are a little bit more interesting. But it's beans with everything, even in the bread.

The most exciting moment is when we eat a thin piece of sausage once a week, and put some jam on our bread – no butter, of course! But we're still alive, and much of the time the food tastes good too.

Wednesday, 5 April 1944

For a long time now, I haven't really been interested in my schoolwork. The end of the war still seemed so far away. And if it isn't over by September, I won't go back to school, since I don't want to be two years behind.

Peter filled my days, nothing but Peter. Nothing but dreams and thoughts, until Saturday night when I felt terrible. I sat on the floor in my nightdress and said my prayers. Then I just lay down on the floor and cried. But I knew I had to fight against it and, finally, when I climbed back into bed at ten o'clock, the suffering was over!

And now it's really over. I've realized that I must do my schoolwork. I want to make something of my life. I want to be a journalist. I *know* I can write. A few of my stories are good, a lot of my diary is alive and amusing, but . . . I don't know yet if I can be a really good writer. But then if I can't write books or for newspapers, I can always write for myself. I don't want to live like Mother, Mrs van Daan, and all the other women who simply do their work and are then forgotten. I need more than just a husband and children! I want to be useful, and to bring enjoyment to all people, even those that I've never met. I want to go on living after my death!

I'm grateful to God for my writing. So I'll go on trying, and everything will be all right, because I'm not going to give up!

Tuesday, 11 April 1944

I don't know where to start – so much has happened. Thursday, when I wrote to you, everything was as usual. Friday and Saturday too. Then on Sunday evening at nine-thirty, Peter knocked at our door. He asked Father to come upstairs and help him with some English words. But I didn't believe him.

'That's strange,' I said to Margot. 'I think we've got burglars.'

I was right. They were breaking into the warehouse at that moment. Father, Mr van Daan and Peter went downstairs as quickly as possible. Margot, Mother, Mrs van Daan and I waited. Four frightened women need to talk, so that's what we did. Then we heard a loud noise, but nobody came back until ten o'clock.

Anne, Amsterdam, 1941.

Father looked quite white when he came in to us. 'Lights out, and get upstairs quietly! The police will be here soon!'

The men went back downstairs, so we still didn't know what had happened. But ten minutes later they were back. They told us that burglars broke down the warehouse door and that Mr van Daan had shouted 'Police!' They tried to put the door back, but the burglars kicked it down again. Then a man and a woman on the street shone a lamp in from the street. (We later found out that this was Mr van Hoeven, the man who brings us potatoes, and his wife.)

We waited and waited in the dark until after eleven o'clock. Then there was more noise downstairs, and finally someone tried to move the bookcase. We were so frightened. I thought the police were going to take us away. But then the person went away, and the house was quiet. We had to stay quiet all night too, and use a large tin for a toilet. We tried to sleep on the floor.

'We should hide the radio!' said Mrs van Daan.

'If they find us, it doesn't matter if they find the radio too,' answered Mr van Daan.

'Then they'll find Anne's diary as well,' said my father.

'So we should burn it!' suggested someone.

Oh, not my diary! If my diary goes, I go too! But fortunately, nothing was done.

At seven, we rang Mr Kleiman, and at last Jan and Miep arrived. They had to go off again to the police to inform them about the burglars, so we had half an hour to tidy up the house and get everything straight. It was an awful smelly mess!

We were in terrible danger that night. Just think, the police were by the bookcase, but they didn't find us. God was truly watching over us. 'You have saved us, please save us in the future!' That's what our prayer is now.

From now on, we must be more careful too. Dussel will do his work in the bathroom, and Peter will walk round the house between eight-thirty and nine-thirty every evening. Somebody noticed that Peter's window was open, so he must keep it shut now.

It has reminded us that we are Jews, and that we must live like prisoners. We must forget our personal feelings and be brave and strong. One day this terrible war will be over. The time will come when we'll be people again and not just Jews!

Who has made us suffer like this? Who has separated us from all the other people? God has made us like this, but God will lift us up again. Perhaps afterwards, if there are any Jews left, our suffering will teach people something. Perhaps they will learn something about goodness, and this is why we have to suffer. We can never be just Dutch, or just English – we will always be Jews as well.

Be brave! There will be a way out. God has always looked after us. All through history, Jews have had to suffer, but there are still Jews, and the suffering has made us stronger.

I thought that I was going to die that night. I waited for death like a soldier. But now that I'm still alive, I want to stay in Holland after the war. I love the Dutch, I love this country, I love the language. I want to work here.

If God lets me live, I will do more than Mother ever did. I want my voice to be heard! I'll go out into the world and work for all human beings!

Sunday, 16 April 1944

Remember yesterday's date, because it was special for me. When a girl gets her first kiss, it's always an important date.

Last night, I was sitting with Peter on his sofa-bed, and he soon put his arm around me. I put my arm round him too, and we sat very close. We've sat like this before, but never as close as we were

43

last night. He wanted me to put my head on his shoulder, then he rested his head on mine. Oh, it was so wonderful! He touched my cheek, my arm and my hair.

At nine-thirty we stood up to go – Peter had to check the building. I was standing next to him. I must have made the right movement, I don't know how, because he gave me a kiss. It was a kiss through my hair, half on my left cheek, and half on my ear. I ran downstairs and didn't look back!

Friday, 28 April 1944

Last night, Peter and I were sitting on the sofa as usual, in each other's arms. Suddenly, the usual Anne disappeared – the confident, noisy Anne – and the second Anne took her place. This second Anne only wants to love and to be gentle. Tears came to my eyes. Did he notice? He made no movement. Did he feel the same way as I did? He said very little. There were no answers to my questions.

At eight-thirty I stood up and went to the window, where we always say goodbye. I was still Anne number two. He came over to me, and I threw my arms around his neck and kissed him on his left cheek. I was going to kiss his other cheek too, when my mouth met his, and we kissed each other again and again!

Last night was a great shock to my heart. The gentle Anne doesn't appear very often, and she's not going to go away quickly. Oh Peter, what have you done to me? What do you want from me?

But if I was older and he wanted to marry me, what would I say? Anne, be honest! I couldn't marry him. Peter isn't strong enough as a person. He's still a child.

Tuesday, 2 May 1944

On Saturday night I asked Peter whether I should tell Father about us. He thinks that I should. I was glad; it means that he's sensible. As soon as I came downstairs, I went with Father to get some water.

While we were on the stairs I said, 'Father, when Peter and I are together, we don't exactly sit at opposite ends of the room. But you've probably guessed that. Do you think that's wrong?'

Father paused for a moment, then answered, 'No, I don't think it's wrong. But Anne, when you're living so close together as we do, you have to be careful.'

Later, on Sunday morning, he said more to me about it. 'You must be the one to be careful – it's the man who always wants to go further. In the outside world, it's different. You're free, you see other boys and girls, and you can play sport and do a lot of different things. But here, you see each other every hour of the day. Be careful Anne, and don't take it too seriously!'

Father says that I shouldn't go upstairs so often, but I still want to. Yes, I'm going!

Wednesday, 3 May 1944

For the last two weeks, we've been eating lunch at eleven-thirty on Saturdays. From tomorrow, it'll be like that every day. That will be one meal less each day. It's still very hard to get vegetables. This afternoon we ate some bad cooked lettuce. Add some bad potatoes, and you have a meal fine enough for a king!

I haven't had my period for more than two months, but it finally started last Sunday. Although it's a trouble and a mess, I'm glad.

You can imagine we often say, 'Why are there wars? Why, oh why, can't people live together peacefully?'

No one can give a really good answer. Why is England making bigger and better aeroplanes and bombs, and at the same time also building new houses? Why do governments give millions each day for war, when they spend nothing on medicine or poor people? Why must people go without food, when there are mountains of food going bad in other parts of the world? Oh, why are people so crazy?

It's not only governments who make war. No, the common man is guilty too! We give our governments the authority to do it. There's something in people that makes them murder and kill. Unless all human beings change, there will still be wars.

I'm often sad here, but I still see our life in the Secret Annexe as an adventure. It's dangerous but exciting. I've decided that I want to live a different kind of life, not like other girls, and that I won't be an ordinary housewife. Living here is an interesting beginning to my life, and that's why I laugh at the amusing side of it, even when it's dangerous.

I'm young, and I'm strong, happy and cheerful. I feel that I'm growing up more every day, and that the end of the war is not far away. Nature is still beautiful, and the people around me are good. Every day, I think what an interesting adventure this is! So why be sad or frightened?

Saturday, 6 May 1944

It is hard to believe it when Jan, Mr Kugler and Mr Kleiman tell us about the prices of food in the outside world. Everything is so expensive, and people buy and sell on the black market. One person can sell you a little bit of wool, another some ration books, and another some cheese. Stealing and murder happen every day.

Even the police and the night watchmen are doing it. Everyone wants food to put in their stomachs, and they can't earn enough money to eat.

Monday, 8 May 1944

Have I ever told you anything about my family? I don't think I have, so let me begin. Father was born in Frankfurt-am-Main, and his parents were very rich. Michael Frank, his father, owned a bank. When Father was young, there were parties and dances every week, and they lived in an enormous house. But when his father died, most of the money was lost, and after the Great War and the problems in Germany, there was nothing left at all.

Mother's family wasn't so rich, but they had quite a lot of money, and she also tells us stories of private dances and parties with 250 guests.

We're not at all rich now, but I hope things will be good after the war. I'd like to spend a year in Paris and London, to learn the languages and study art history. I've told you before, I want to see the world and do all kinds of exciting things! And a little money will be very useful!

Friday, 19 May 1944

I felt awful yesterday. I was sick, and had a headache. I'm feeling better today. I'm very hungry, but I won't eat the beans that we're having for dinner.

Everything is going fine between Peter and me. We kiss each other goodnight every evening, and he always asks for another kiss. He's so happy to know that somebody loves him!

I'm not so close to him now as I was. My love hasn't grown

colder, though. Peter's a lovely boy, but I've closed the door to the Anne deep inside. If he wants to find her again, he'll have to break down the door!

Monday, 22 May 1944

We've heard something very sad and frightening. It seems that a lot of people are thinking differently about us Jews now. People are against us who were once totally on our side. Some Christians are saying that the Jews tell secrets to the Germans. They say that the Jews are telling the authorities about their helpers, and then those people are arrested. And then, of course, the punishments that they get are terrible. Yes, it's all true. But they should ask themselves this: if Christians were in our place, would they behave differently? Could anyone, Jew or Christian, stay silent when the Germans are trying to make them talk? Everyone knows that it's almost impossible, so why do they ask us, the Jews, to do something impossible?

I have only one hope: that the Dutch will not be against us for long. They should remember again in their hearts what's right, because this isn't right at all.

Thursday, 25 May 1944

Something happens every day now. This morning they arrested Mr van Hoeven, the man who brings the potatoes. He was helping two Jews, who were hiding in his house. The world is turned upside down. The best people are in concentration camps and prisons, while the worst decide to put them there. It's terrible for Mr van Hoeven, and for those poor Jews. It's also very difficult for us. Bep can't possibly carry all those heavy potatoes, so we'll

48

have to eat less of them. Mother says that we won't eat breakfast; lunch will be bread and something simple; and dinner will be potatoes. If possible, we'll eat vegetables or lettuces once or twice a week. That's all there is.

Monday, 5 June 1944

There are new problems in the Annexe now. There's a quarrel between Dussel and the Franks. We can't agree how to share out the butter.

Then the van Daans don't agree that we should make a cake for Mr Kugler's birthday when we can't have one ourselves. It's all very silly. Mood upstairs: bad. Mrs van Daan has a cold.

The weather is awful. The Allies are bombing the Pas de Calais and the west coast of France.

No one is buying American dollars now, and they aren't interested in gold either. We shall soon come to the bottom of our black money-box. How will we have enough money to live next month?

Tuesday, 6 June 1944

'This is D-Day,' the BBC said on the radio at twelve o'clock. 'This is *the* day.' The invasion has begun!

The German news says that British soldiers have arrived on the coast of France, and are fighting the Germans there.

At one o'clock the BBC said that 11,000 planes are flying in to help the invasion. They're carrying soldiers, or on bombing raids. 4,000 boats are arriving on the coast between Cherbourg and Le Havre. British and American armies are already fighting there.

We can't believe it! Is this really the beginning of the end of the war? We've talked about it so much – but it still seems too good to be true! Will they win the war this year, in 1944? We don't know yet. But where there's hope, there's life. It makes us brave and strong again.

Now that the invasion has started, I feel that friends are coming! Maybe, Margot says, I can even go back to school in September or October!

Friday, 9 June 1944

Great news of the invasion! The Allies have taken Bayeux, a village on the coast of France. They're now fighting for the town of Caen.

Tuesday, 13 June 1944

I've had another birthday, so now I'm fifteen. I had quite a few presents; among them were an art history book, some underwear, a handkerchief, a pot of jam, two small honey cakes, a book about plants from Mother and Father, sweets from Miep, and some lovely flowers from Peter.

The invasion is still going well, although the weather is terrible – heavy rain, strong winds and rough seas.

Peter loves me more each day, but something is holding us back, and I don't know what it is. Sometimes I wonder if I wanted him too much; I think that perhaps it wasn't real. But then if I can't go up to his room for a day or two, I want him badly again. Peter is kind and good, but in some ways I'm not happy about him as a person. He doesn't think much of God, for example, and I don't like the way that he talks about food. And why doesn't he let me come close to him, really close to the person deep inside him?

I haven't been outside for so long that everything in the natural world seems wonderful to me now. I remember a time when I didn't notice the blue sky, or the flowers, or hear the song of the birds. All that has changed. When I can, I try to watch the moon, or the dark, rainy sky through our windows. And when I look at the clouds, the moon and the stars, I really do feel calm and hopeful. It's the best medicine, and I am stronger afterwards.

Unfortunately, I usually have to try and look through dusty curtains and very dirty windows.

Tuesday, 27 June 1944

The mood has changed, and everything outside is going very well. The Allies have won Cherbourg, Vitebsk and Zhlobin. In the three weeks since D-Day, there have been rain and storms every day, but the British and the Americans have fought hard.

How far do you think we'll be on 27 July?

Saturday, 15 July 1944

I know that I won Peter as a friend, not the other way round. I was the one who tried to make it work. And I made a picture of him in my mind as a quiet, sweet boy who badly needed a loving friend. I needed someone to talk to, to say what was in my heart. I wanted a friend too, who would help me to find my way again. I succeeded; slowly but surely, he came towards me. Finally, we became friends, but we became very close too. I find it hard to believe now that we grew so close! We talked about very private things, but never about what was deep in my heart. And I still can't understand Peter. Is he really shy, or is there nothing deep in him at all?

263 Prinsengracht, Amsterdam. Seen from the rear.

But I made one big mistake. I wanted him to be close to me, and now we can't be friends any other way. And he's holding on to me too tightly. I can't see how to change this now.

Friday, 21 July 1944

Now, at last, things are going well! Great news! Somebody tried to kill Hitler, and it was actually a German army official who tried to do it! This shows us that many of the German soldiers have had enough of the war too, and would like to end it.

Tuesday, 1 August 1944

I'm two people, really, as I've often told you. One side of me is cheerful and amusing, and enjoys a kiss or a rude joke. This is the Anne that people know, and they will be amused by me for an afternoon, but after that they've had enough of me for a month! No one knows the other side, the better side of Anne. It's deeper and finer. But the first Anne always shows herself, and won't let the second Anne out. I try, but it doesn't work. It's because I'm afraid – afraid that people will laugh at me. Of course people laugh at me now – I'm used to it – but they laugh at the amusing 'lighthearted' Anne. She doesn't care, but the 'deeper' Anne is too weak for that. If I make the good Anne come out even for fifteen minutes, she won't speak, and allows Anne number one to talk. Then, before I realize it, she's disappeared again.

So the nice Anne never comes out in front of other people, but she's almost always there when I'm alone. I would like to change, and I'm trying hard, but it's difficult. If I'm quiet and serious, my family thinks I'm ill! But I keep trying to become what I would like to be, and what I could be if ... if only there were no other people in the world.

ANNE'S DIARY ENDS HERE

AFTERWORD

On the morning of 4 August 1944, a car arrived at 263 Prinsengracht, the address of the Secret Annexe. German and Dutch police arrested the eight people who were hiding in the Annexe. Somebody must have told the authorities that they were hiding there. They also arrested two of their helpers, Mr Kugler and Mr Kleiman. Miep and Bep were not arrested. The police took all the money and anything valuable that they could find in the Annexe. Miep later found Anne's diary in the building and kept it safely until after the war.

The police took Kugler and Kleiman to a prison in Amsterdam. On 11 September 1944 they were sent to a concentration camp in Amersfoot, also in Holland. Because Kleiman was ill, he was allowed to go free on 18 September. He lived in Amsterdam until he died in 1959.

Kugler later escaped, and he went to live in Canada, where he died in 1989.

Bep's real name was Elisabeth Voskuijl Wijk, and she died in Amsterdam in 1983.

Miep Santrouschitz Gies is still living in Amsterdam, but her husband Jan died in 1993.

The eight people from the Annexe were first taken to a prison in Amsterdam. Then they were sent to Auschwitz, the concentration camp in Poland.

It seems that Mr van Daan died by gas at Auschwitz, and his wife was taken to several more concentration camps. She died in a concentration camp, though nobody knows exactly how. On 16 January 1945, Peter van Daan had to go on the terrible prisoners' walk from Auschwitz to Mauthausen in Austria, where he died on 5 May 1945. He died only three days before the Allies got to the camp.

Albert Dussel died on 20 December 1944 in the Neuen Gamme concentration camp.

Edith Frank, Anne's mother, died in the Auschwitz concentration camp on 6 January 1945, too tired and too hungry to live any longer.

Margot and Anne Frank were taken from Auschwitz to the Bergen–Belsen concentration camp near Hanover, in Germany. A terrible illness attacked the prisoners there. They both died in the winter of 1944–5. Anne must have died in late February or early March. All the bodies of the prisoners were thrown together. The British army arrived at the camp on 12 April 1945.

Otto Frank was the only one of the eight still alive. After Russian soldiers reached Auschwitz, he was finally taken back to Amsterdam. In 1953, he moved to Switzerland, married again, and lived there until his death in 1980. He spent the rest of his life trying to share the message of his daughter's diary with the rest of the world.

EXERCISES

Vocabulary Work

Check each Dictionary Word and make sure that you know what it means.

1 Write sentences using the following pairs of words:

   a suffer/prayer

   b share/cheerful

   c store/bookcase

   d quarrel/allowed

2 Here are three words used about buildings. Write sentences to show the meaning of each.

   a warehouse

   b annexe

   c attic

3 Some words in this book are used mostly in wartime. Write a sentence for each one, showing that you understand the meaning.

   a raid

   b allies

   c invasion

   d concentration camp

4 Which words mean the same as:

   a to keep things like food or clothes safely?

   b the monthly change in a woman's body?

   c the government or its officials?

   d to take someone away and put them in prison?

   e facts about the past?

Comprehension

Look in the diary to find the answers to these questions. On questions 1–8 use the dates to help you:

June 1942
1 Why did the Frank family move from Germany to Holland?
2 When and in what way did things get worse for them in Holland?

From July–November 1942
3 Where did they decide to hide?
4 Why was it called 'The Secret Annexe'?
5 Who hid there?

July 1943
6 What dangerous things were happening on the streets of Amsterdam?
7 What dangerous thing happened in the Annexe?

February and June 1944
8 What did people think would happen soon in the war?

Life in the Annexe
9 Describe different ways in which the Frank family heard news from the outside world.
10 Where did their food come from?
11 What did Anne want to do with her life when she grew up?
12 When and how did their life in the Secret Annexe end?

Discussion

1 What problems were there for the eight people who were trying to live together? How would you try to solve them?

2   What did they do to:
    a try and enjoy life?
    b look after their health?
    c keep their minds lively?
    What would you do?
 3 Do you think Anne changes in the story? Say how you think she changes, or why you don't think she changes.
 4 Do you think Anne and Peter really fell in love? Say why or why not.

Writing

Either: Write a short newspaper report (150 words) about the final arrest of the people from the Annexe. Say who was there, how they lived and who helped them.

Or: You are Anne, and you want to describe your room in your diary. Write about what you have there, who you share it with and what happens there (250 words). Use any information that you like from the diary. Look at the plan of the Annexe to help you.

Review

 1 Why do you think Anne's diary has become so famous?
 2 Do you think that it is only a sad book, or that it gives us hope for the future?
 3 Do you like Anne as a person? Do you think she is an unusual girl? Say why or why not.